MORE THAN ORDINARY

marriage:

a higher level

KIT AND DREW COONS

More Than Ordinary Marriage: A Higher Level

© 2018 Kit and Drew Coons

ISBN: 978-0-9995689-6-5

Unless otherwise noted, all Scripture quotations are taken from the New American Standard Bible (NASB). Copyright © 1960, 1962, 1963, 1968, 1971, 1972, 1973, 1975, 1977, 1995 by The Lockman Foundation

Edited by Jayna Richardson
Design: Julie Sullivan (MerakiLifeDesigns.com)

First Edition
Printed in the United States

22 21 20 19 18   1 2 3 4 5

contents

Contents

WHAT IS A MORE THAN ORDINARY
marriage?
_____

Some might suggest that any marriage that survives in these times is more than ordinary. Unfortunately, many marriages don't last a lifetime. But by "more than ordinary," we mean a marriage that does more than survive and is even more than successful. A more than ordinary marriage can cause others to ask, "What makes their relationship so special?"

"I don't know what we can learn about marriage," said the chairman of the deacons at a church retreat. "We've been married 43 years." A smattering of applause congratulated him and his wife. Then for the rest of that retreat the older couple demonstrated what you don't want your marriage to be after 43 years. Having a poor marriage isn't God's plan any more than getting a divorce. Sadly, even many in the church fail to realize or demonstrate the fullness of marriage God intends.

Sometimes couples ask us, "If you could tell us just one marriage principle, the most important, what would that be?"

We respond, "The single most important principle is a commitment to having a good marriage, not just a commitment to staying married." Then we add, "And the second most important principle is to develop a common plan for your marriage."

We illustrate the plan's importance as a blueprint. "How would two carpenters building a house do if they worked from different blueprints?" Different ideas held by a husband and wife are at the root of most marriage difficulties. But developing a common plan is hard and sometimes discouraging work. That's why the commitment to having a good marriage comes first. Couples need commitment to a good marriage to develop and implement the plan.

Fortunately, the Bible provides principles that can help a couple formulate a common plan. Most marriage teaching focuses on foundational principles to help marriages be successful. Applying biblical principles on forgiveness, communication, acceptance, "leave, cleave, and become one flesh," conflict resolution, and intimacy can help a couple establish a common plan for a successful marriage.

This mini-book will assume that those foundational principles for a successful marriage have already been applied. Some foundational principles such as dealing with conflict, especially in a stressful difficulty, are touched on in *More Than Ordinary Challenges: Dealing with the Unexpected*.[1] But this text will go beyond them to discuss biblical principles that can give a couple a more than ordinary marriage. This can truly honor God for the following reasons:

1. Marriage Illustrates Christ and the Church

The Apostle Paul in Ephesians 5:23-32 illustrates Christ and the church using the relationship between a husband and wife. In verse 32, he calls it a "mystery." Not all has been explained. But certainly marriages are a key part of God's purposes. Our marriage isn't just for us. A more than ordinary marriage reflects God's character.

2. Love is the Greatest Commandment

"He (Jesus) said to him, 'You shall love the Lord your God with all your heart, and with all your soul, and with all your mind.' This is the great and foremost commandment. The second is like it, 'You shall love your neighbor as yourself.' On these two commandments depend the whole Law and the Prophets." (Matthew 22:37-40) Our spouse is our closest neighbor. Truly loving them as ourselves is second only to loving God.

3. Marriage is the crucible in which God can make us like Jesus

Drew: Kit and I had started leading Bible discussion groups on marriage to help ourselves and other couples. The first lesson concerned controlling selfishness in marriage. I concentrated every day on trying to be a less selfish husband. At my workplace, a coworker came into my office. "Drew, what you did for those guys was really unselfish," he said.

"Wow!" I thought. "My marriage has spilled over into other parts of my life!" As I worked to be a less selfish husband, God also used that to make me a less selfish person.

This is part of God's purpose for marriage. Marriage can be the crucible in which our Christianity can be purified. As I continued to work to become a better husband, God made me a better Christian.

A more than ordinary marriage is also part of discipleship. Our observation is that most Christian churches and organizations put a lot of emphasis on a form of "discipleship" that rarely includes marriage enrichment. Of course, part of the reason is so that the emphasis will be inclusive of those not married. But husbands and wives can have a special discipleship advantage by helping each other to be better Christians. This mini-book will show how.

Who said, "A man shall leave his mother and father, and cleave to his wife, and the two shall become one flesh?" Was that Moses, Jesus, or Paul? As a matter of fact, all three of these very important men in the Bible emphasized this principle. When these three highlight the same exact value, it deserves a strategic place within "discipleship."

Another essential aspect of discipleship is to pass along biblical principles to others. "Go therefore and make disciples of all the nations, baptizing them in the name of the Father and the Son and the Holy Spirit, teaching them to observe all that I commanded you; and lo, I am with you always, even to the end of the age." (Matthew 28:19-20) "The things which you have heard from me in the presence of many witnesses, entrust these to faithful men who will be able to teach others also." (2 Timothy 2:2)

God's character is on display in marriage. By simply having a more than ordinary marriage, couples will be teaching others by example. Most couples who came to our ministry usually hoped for more than instruction. They sought role models — couples making their relationship work, despite difficulties. And what's wrong with that? Not a thing! The Apostle Paul wrote, "Join in following my example, and observe those who walk according to the pattern you have in us." (Philippians 3:17) Being an example is a strong aspect of biblical discipleship and works especially well in the context of marriage.

This mini-book will explore biblical ideas by which marriages can be more than ordinary, providing the greatest satisfaction for the couple and honoring God.

SACRIFICIAL
serving

Scripture tells men to "love your wives." Asked how to love one's wife, Christian men often recite Ephesians 5:25, "Just as Christ also loved the church and gave Himself up for her." They often conclude, "A husband gives up his life for his wife and children like Jesus did for the church." A correct theological answer. But what does this look like in a marriage? Most husbands would fight, would lay down their lives if necessary, to defend their wife and children were they in danger. Fortunately, that is a rare necessity. We are, however, asked to give up pieces of our lives. Doing things around the house, going shopping, taking care of the children, or just listening are all examples of loving as Christ does the church. This is sacrificial service.

> Drew: I hate mowing grass. For me, when you can't see the lawn furniture anymore, that's the time to cut

the grass. As newlyweds, Kit and I purchased a house with an acre of grass. Immediately I started converting the yard into woods. Trees and bushes would come right up to the house. Kit pleaded, "Every nice home needs grass." My answer: "You want grass? Then you'll cut it!" For years, Kit did our grass cutting. On hot afternoons, I would be watching a ball game on TV while my young wife mowed grass. Yes, I did that. Then I learned more about being a biblical servant-leader. Changes needed to be made! So, I bought her a lawnmower with a bagger. Well, that was a step in the right direction. But to be a godly husband, I eventually started cutting the grass.

Galatians 5:13 and other scriptures tell us to "serve one another." A servant does the dirty jobs. The jobs he doesn't want to do. Generally, wives, especially mothers, are more inherently service oriented. Many Christian teachers talk to wives about submission. Often wives internally translate "submission" as "I get stuck with all the dirty jobs." Wives find submitting a lot easier when their husbands are sacrificially serving them by putting her needs above his own.

Drew: So, do you want to be a real man? Are you willing to accept a really tough challenge? Try out-serving your wife. And for those who emphasize the headship of husbands, serving is your job more than hers. "Whoever wishes to become great among you shall be your servant." (Matthew 20:26)

But I've got a warning. Your wives are smart. They'll know what you're doing. She may think, "That guy is trying to out-serve me. He won't get away with that." She'll serve you more. Then you'll have to serve her even more to stay ahead. You may find yourselves in an upward spiral of serving one another. That's when marriage becomes more than ordinary.

And you may find some unexpected results. One day, I noticed a little dirt on the kitchen floor. I was sweeping it up when Kit came in. "You are so sexy with that broom," she said. My response? "Then wait until you see me with the vacuum cleaner."

Blessing for an Insult

All of us say or do things that hurt our spouses. Forgiveness is an essential part of a successful marriage. Sacrificially serving goes a step further. In 1 Peter 3:9, we're exhorted, "Not returning evil for evil or insult for insult, but giving a blessing instead."

A couple had been arguing when the husband said to the wife, "How could God have made you so beautiful and so dumb!" The wife replied, "The reason God made me so beautiful was so that you would love me. And the reason He made me so dumb was so I would love you!" That's an insult for an insult!

Kit: As we all know, hurt in marriage is inevitable. The question is how are we going to respond? Maybe you can relate to my experience: Drew comes home from work frustrated from a job-related problem. He starts, "Have you done the errands? Have you fed the dogs? Have you cut the grass? All you ever do is sit around!"

I have two ways I can respond to this. Unfortunately, I usually respond like this: "Well, have you done even ONE thing on that list I gave you? You never do anything around here. I have to do everything by myself." What happened? Drew insulted me, and I insulted him right back.

But Scripture calls us to give a blessing for an insult. The best way for me to respond would be to answer Drew's questions. Not pout, at which I'm very adept. And try to enjoy the rest of the evening. In other words, let it go. And the blessing I could give Drew would be to get out the rolling pin. No, not to hit him over the head with it. But to make him biscuits because they are his favorite food.

Sounds impossible, doesn't it? In our own strength, giving a blessing for an insult would be. But Jesus said, "All things are possible with God." (Mark 10:27) Sacrificially serving one another by giving a blessing for an insult can revolutionize a relationship.

GENUINE
encouragement

Drew: As a young Christian, I wanted to grow in Christ. I had a godly pastor whom I respected. But I felt he never took enough time for me—not as much time as I'd like, anyway. And my pastor had good reason. He had 300 other families to care for, not to mention his own. But I found myself wishing, "Wouldn't it be great if you could have your own minister, someone to help you be all God would have you to be?" Years later I found out that is exactly God's plan. And the minister He appointed for me is my wife, Kit. And I'm to be her minister. That's part of God's plan for marriage. However, the manner we can minister to each other is *not by preaching, but by encouraging one another.*

Therefore, encourage one another and build up one another, just as you also are doing. (1 Thessalonians 5:11)

Encouragement isn't telling a person what you think they should do, a "You can do it!" pep talk, or false praise. Real encouragement begins with discovering and praising what a person does well. Remember the Proverbs 31 wife? Her abilities added a lot to her family's daily welfare. Ever notice her husband's response? The Bible records that he sat in the gates of the city and publicly praised his wife. Was the praise his response to her ability? Or was her ability a response to his praise? Certainly, the two responses nurture each other. If you want a better husband or wife, learn to sincerely encourage the one you have.

Drew: Competitive tennis was a big part of my life for twenty years. Since I played a lot, Kit took up the game as well. As she started to improve, she had an idea: "We could have fun playing doubles against other couples." Now, that can be a test of anybody's marriage. You know how engaged couples go through pre-marital counseling? I think they should play tennis together to learn how their future spouse might respond under pressure.

The problem was that I wanted to win more than

anything. People play tennis for fun, right? Well, losing was no fun for me. Therefore, when we started playing together, I began telling Kit mistakes she was making on the court. I pointed out lots of ways she ought to improve her game.

To my surprise, she started playing poorly. As I continued telling her everything she needed to do differently, she played even worse. Nearly every time she could touch the ball with her racket, the other side got a point. Finally, in one match I told her, "Serve the ball and step off the court. I'll play them by myself."

But I couldn't win that way. Kit didn't literally leave the court, but she really was out of that match. Our opponents could hit the ball past me down the sideline. I had to ask Kit to cover the line so that I could win. She did, and we came from behind to win.

That day I started to discover the power of godly encouragement. The way Kit played tennis was directly related to the way I treated her on the court. Whenever I started to criticize her, she was awful. But when I sincerely encouraged her, she was a great player. Her game was nearly 100% determined by my words.

Most of us tend to underestimate the power of our words. We first recognized that on the tennis court. But then like the Proverbs 31 husband we learned how to use words to help each other in many areas. Most important, we found that encouragement can do the work of God in our spouse's life. When we praise godly qualities like patience, thoughtfulness, hospitality, and generosity, our spouse is thusly motivated. By such encouragement, we help them to focus on the good things that determine the quality of a person's life. Doing so, we become a minister to our spouse.

> *Whatever is true, whatever is honorable, whatever is right, whatever is pure, whatever is lovely, whatever is of good repute, if there is any excellence and if anything worthy of praise, dwell on these things. (Philippians 4:8)*

An extra powerful way to encourage our spouses is to look for opportunities to praise them in public. Public compliments such as those the Proverbs 31 husband demonstrated are the most effective. Proverbs 25:11 says, "Like apples of gold in settings of silver is a word spoken in right circumstances." Well-chosen words of praise spoken in public are one of the greatest gifts we can give our spouses.

As you seek to encourage your spouse, there are a couple of actions to avoid. One thing you don't need to do is lie or grossly exaggerate, such as, "The mashed potatoes are wonderful. How did you make them so chewy?" When we falsify our compliments, we undermine our credibility. "You are the most beautiful woman in the world," may cause doubt as to our sincerity. "I think you are so beautiful," is sufficient.

Secondly, never criticize or joke in front of others at your spouse's expense. We've seen many men and women trying to get a laugh in a social situation by telling about something silly their spouse did. Your spouse may laugh along, but your words hurt them inside. Doing so, you fail to minister and assist them to become all God intends.

Biblical Self-Esteem through Respect

Showing respect is another form of encouragement. What a person thinks about himself is important. The Bible says, "As he thinks within himself, so he is." (Proverbs 23:7) How we see ourselves determines our concept of self and affects our relationship with God. You might be wondering, "Self-esteem and Christianity? Didn't Jesus teach to die to self? And how does self-esteem relate to marriage?"

Others might think, "My spouse, *more* self-esteem? That's the last thing he (or she) needs. He already thinks too much of himself." But we're not talking about pride. Romans 12:3 says that no one should "think more highly of himself than he ought to think." Biblical self-esteem thinks accurately about ourselves in relation to God. We can help our spouses to acquire biblical self-esteem through respect.

> Kit: Ladies, we need to understand that a man's life is filled with ways he is attempting to gain respect. Whether it's competing with peers at work, driving the fastest car, or catching the biggest fish, a man is

constantly looking for recognition from others. He wants to win because along with the winning comes respect. If we want our spouses to win at home, we need to give them respect.

We're not talking about building up egos. Rather, we are talking about having a positive perspective and being honest about who we are before God. This perspective will give the confidence that God can do great things through us. Numbers 12:3 says, "Now the man Moses was very humble, more than any man who was on the face of the earth." And yet Moses developed the confidence to speak to God face-to-face as a man does to his friend. And God used Moses to do great things. Being sincerely respected leads to true humility and great accomplishments.

honoring

Christians should honor each other. A literal translation of Romans 12:10 from an older NASB version says, "Outdo one another in showing honor." Husbands in particular are instructed to honor their wives: "Show her honor as a fellow heir of the grace of life, so that your prayers will not be hindered." (1 Peter 3:7)

> *And those members of the body which we deem less honorable, on these we bestow more abundant honor, and our less presentable members become much more presentable. (1 Corinthians 12:23)*

Sometimes our spouses may feel inadequate or "less presentable." This is the occasion to give them more honor. Honor is recognition of what a person has done and of his or her God-given talents. Honoring means considering the other as God's creation and an important part of His plan for your life.

We can honor our spouses in several ways:

Identifying and Maximizing Strengths

Each man has his own gift from God, one in this manner, and another in that. (1 Corinthians 7:7)

Discovering your spouse's strengths and maximizing them is part of honoring. Start with the assurance that God has bestowed on your spouse special gifts and talents different from your own gifts and talents. Positively identifying differences is also part of God's plan to make you stronger as a team.

Receiving acknowledgment of strength in one area can give a person confidence to improve in other areas. In amateur tennis doubles, usually the stronger player is given the left or backhand side. We discovered that Kit could consistently hit the ball safely across court from left to right. We gave her the left side. Kit then learned to lob the ball effectively. She thereby neutralized aggressive opponents who charged the net. After Kit's lob, as we scrambled backwards, I (Drew) would shift to cut off their return angle. Soon Kit's other tennis shots became strong enough that we could switch our positions on the court in the middle of a point. This really confused our opponents. We had identified and maximized our individual strengths, which led to each of us learning new skills.

Honoring also allows us to accept and minimize weaknesses we discover. For example, Kit just didn't have the upper body strength to hit an overhead smash. Once I accepted that, we agreed that she would step aside, and I would smash the ball when the opportunity came. Honoring on the tennis court allowed us to beat teams that had more talent.

Drew: After I learned how to honor Kit on the tennis court, she played better and better. She became so good that we played in a tennis league one summer where she was the only woman. All the other players were men who, like me, wanted to win. We played for a position on our team and won a starting spot. Together we won over half of our matches. I never had so much fun playing tennis as that summer with Kit. I found that losing with Kit was more fun than winning with anybody else. And the fun was made possible because we had learned how to identify and maximize our strengths.

Although the tennis was fun, it ultimately served as our training ground for difficult ministry together. Knowing how to honor each other allowed us to develop a Christian marriage ministry together in our area that involved nearly 10,000 couples.

Drew: Like in tennis, we had different strengths and weaknesses. For example, in many places, we were asked to give radio or TV interviews. When asked an unexpected question, Kit can freeze, not knowing what to say. I can quickly think of an answer usually extracted from materials we've written. Unfortunately, my slow speech and southern accent make me sound like my mouth is full of cotton. But with her beautiful mid-western voice, Kit can communicate clearly. Therefore, we learned that I should respond first giving an idea and then pause. Kit could then answer more fully and clearly.

Freedom to Fail

There is no fear in love; but perfect love casts out fear.
(1 John 4:18)

Honoring your spouse involves assurance of unconditional love and forgiveness in times of failure. In our culture, if you are not successful by the measuring stick of society, you feel like a failure. But the truth is, we all fail on occasion. How our spouses help or hinder us during times of failure can have a major impact on our lives.

Kit: Although Drew and I share the failure to have children, it affected my view of myself more than it affected Drew. We went through many years of trying everything you can think of, and more, to have children. We experienced month after month of hope and then despair. My self-confidence was never very solid, but when I had to face infertility, it took a real nose dive. Drew's love and ministry to me during that time, as well as his continual focus on godly character, was my mainstay. Without it, I would have drowned.

Perfect love also creates an environment in which your spouse feels the freedom to try new things and develop new talents. Failures will not stop your spouse from ultimately succeeding. But fear of failure will stop him or her from succeeding. However, you can help take away your spouse's fear.

Drew: As a research engineer, I learned that most attempts to create an invention fail. Failure is just part of the process. Without being willing to fail, we can never succeed.

There is a remarkable story in 1 Samuel 13 and 14. The Philistines had come to reassert their control over Israel. Saul led only about 600 men of Israel out to face the multitude of Philistines. Among the Israelites, only Saul and Jonathan had swords. The others carried farm implements to face the well-equipped enemy. Jonathan proposed to the young man who carried his shield that they alone sneak out to face the enemy. "Perhaps the Lord will work for us," he said. And the young man answered, "Do all that is in your heart; turn yourself, and here I am with you according to your desire." (1 Samuel 14:6-7)

Together they revealed themselves to the Philistines, climbed to face them, and slew about 20. The Philistines started to tremble, then the ground quaked, and the multitude of Philistines started to run away in fear. Some Israelites who had been siding with the Philistines, certainly due to fear, switched back to Saul's army. Other Israelites who had been hiding in the hills came to pursue the fleeing enemy. Israel won a great victory. The young man honored Jonathan by supporting his initiative. When we say to our spouse, "Try it. I'm with you," we honor them and set them up to succeed.

Drew: Even before our wedding, I set aggressive savings goals for us. Although that hadn't been a previous value of Kit's, she wholeheartedly joined the effort. Her support allowed us to pay off a 14% interest home loan in less than seven years. Rather than spend the money previously dedicated to house payments, we exercised the discipline to invest it. Ultimately, I was able to take an 80% cut in pay to do charitable work at age forty-seven.

Some people have an aversion to admitting they're wrong. They may bullheadedly pursue a poor choice because they don't want to admit they made a mistake. Knowing your spouse has granted you the freedom to fail can make reassessing a situation and changing your mind much easier. Admitting a mistake early can thereby help you or your spouse avoid spiraling into worse consequences.

Drew: Although Kit had given me the freedom to fail, she experienced some fear when I proposed saving money by having me perm her hair. Nevertheless, she allowed me to try. Once I discovered that my fingers did not have the motor skills to adequately wrap the curls, I stopped before any solution had been applied.

24

Because I had the freedom to fail, I didn't persist into disaster trying to avoid admitting failure.

Freedom to fail honors your spouse and sets them up for dramatic successes. Giving freedom to fail includes being willing to forgive when failure does happen and assures your spouse of your love even during uncertainties.

Valuing

With humility of mind, regard one another as more important than yourselves. (Philippians 2:3)

Volumes of books have been written about the differences between men and women and their respective needs and desires. Plus, every person has unique values unrelated to gender. You can honor your spouse by understanding and valuing what is important to him or her.

Drew: I had always wanted to go fly-in fishing in Alaska. That's when a float plane takes you into a remote area and leaves you. Well, to plan the trip, I requested lots of literature. Everything Alaska sent to us included a pamphlet entitled, "Beware of bears!" They advised: "In the area you are going, carry a loaded rifle at all times." As Kit noticed the pamphlets, she wanted to know, "Will we be safe?"

"Of course," I reassured her. "They just say that to

protect themselves from lawsuits. We'll be lucky to even catch a glimpse of a bear." So we didn't carry a rifle or pepper spray. We got to Alaska, the airplane left us for five days, and bears were everywhere. Kit even had to face off a bear. Her going to Alaska despite misgivings honored me beyond words by trusting me and enabling me to enjoy something I valued.

Kit: Drew does special things for me, too. One of my favorite memories is of an afternoon in a small Belgian town. We found this cute little café with tables on the town square with lanterns and a canopy over our heads. Rain started pitter-pattering on the canopy as the sun set. Lights flickered in the twilight. I continued talking and talking . . . and Drew listened. This is a special memory for me. Drew's preference would be to get fast food and go on to the next sight. But he enjoyed that special moment with me and for me. He honored my value.

Husbands and wives feel honored when the other appreciates their values.

DYNAMIC
teamwork

———

The word "teamwork" can be used in a lot of different situations. On a sled dog team, one dog leads the way and the others follow. Players on a baseball team each play their own position and throw the ball to teammates. A tug-of-war team pulls on the same rope.

The style of teamwork in your marriage may be different from other marriages. The most successful teamwork is based on the strengths of the individuals and the plan they adopt for their unique relationship. Over the course of a more than ordinary marriage, the form of teamwork might even vary. For example, a husband might work outside the home while his wife cares for their children. Later, when their children are grown, the couple might start a business working together. Regardless, teamwork can make a couple's dream work.

Believe You are Stronger as a Team

As each one has received a special gift, employ it in serving one another. (1 Peter 4:10)

"We are soooo different," many couples have said to us. To which we reply, "Good. The more different you are, the more strengths you have as a team." God accentuated our differences by making us male and female. Plus, everyone has special talents and abilities.

Drew: Kit and I have had the opportunity to do a lot of overseas traveling. Kit always amazes me. After being in a new country for just a few days, I hear her start to greet people in their language. We can go into a restaurant with a menu that I can't read a word of. Kit will say, "Number three is roast pork with potatoes."

Kit: I may be able to pick up the language, but I always have a hard time with the money. When we were in Turkey, the exchange rate was 280,000 lira to one dollar. No matter how hard I tried, I just could never figure it out. I was always asking Drew, "How much does this cost in dollars?" And the amazing part was that he could quickly tell me. I didn't have that skill, but he did.

Drew: As we travel, we like to take public transportation, trains, and buses. We can go into an international train station with all the schedules flipping up on the big board. I have no idea what to do or where to go. Kit will look at the board and say, "Our train leaves in twenty minutes on platform four."

Kit: I may be able to get us to the town we're going to, but once we're there, I'm lost. I just can't read a map. Drew can take a map in a language he doesn't know and get us to the cathedral that we want to visit. He'll say, "It's three blocks west. Four blocks north. And the cathedral will be in the southeast corner of the square."

Using our different strengths, we travel together well. Frequently couples think they can't work together as a team because of their differences. The surprise is that differences can make a couple's teamwork stronger. Think of the legs on a chair. If we were to put those legs close together, how stable would the chair be? But the wider you spread the legs, the more stable and useful the chair is. In the same way, the more different we are as individuals, the more God can use us as a team. The key to teamwork begins with believing you are stronger as a team and respecting each other's abilities.

A Common Mission

To have a more than ordinary marriage, a couple needs a common mission as part of their plan. One wonderful purpose is to raise a family together. But not everybody has children, or perhaps the children have grown up and left home. Could we offer some advice to couples without children to care for?

> One reason parenthood is wonderful is that it brings qualities such as unselfishness and self-sacrifice out of most people. We've got good news! God wants those qualities for you regardless of the challenge (childlessness for us) you face. But many are caught in limbo not knowing what to do with their lives because of their challenge. Whatever your challenge, we urge you to find a God-given purpose. Raising children unites most couples with a common purpose. Couples without children also need a common purpose together as a couple. God can use this purpose to bring the best out of you. We don't want to waste our lives. Each day is a gift from God.[1] (Coons, *More Than Ordinary Challenges*)

For those who do care for children, giving them a mom and dad who truly love each other and have fun together is a great gift. Some parents may say, "Our kids don't leave us any time for each other." A more than ordinary marriage prioritizes the husband/wife relationship. Susan Alexander Yates has said, "A child's security is based not on how much his parents love him, but on how much they love each other."

Teamwork in Ministry

For this reason a man shall leave his father and mother and shall be joined to his wife, and the two shall become one flesh. This mystery is great; but I am speaking with reference to Christ and the church. (Ephesians 5:31-32)

God didn't choose to illustrate Christ and the church as husband and wife by accident. As mentioned earlier, the Bible calls this relationship a "mystery." We don't understand all that God's plan involves. But we do know that God expects Christ and the church to minister together. Since the relationship between the husband and wife should illustrate Christ and the church, we can only conclude that this includes a husband and wife ministering together.

Seeing a husband and wife ministering together is rare in the Christian community. Most frequently, the wife has a place of ministry in the church and the husband has an altogether different area of ministry. One reason is that pastors serve as role models for many. Most are male and minister as their full-time job. Their wives are busy taking care of their homes and children. In addition, men ministering to men and women ministering to women is frequently most appropriate. Even when this is not the case, it is rare to see pastoral couples ministering together. 1 Corinthians 14:34 says, "The women are to keep silent in the churches." Some groups in their willingness to be obedient have excluded or limited nearly all ministry opportunities for women. We won't enter the debate about women's role in the church. But we do believe that one unrealized opportunity for both men and women is ministering as a couple.

We started a lay marriage ministry in South Carolina using small-group Bible discussions. In the beginning, we followed the ministry roles we had observed. Kit made the refreshments and I (Drew) conducted the Bible discussion. But during the studies, we soon discovered the advantages of sharing the discussion leadership. For one thing, the one not currently leading could more readily observe the body language of the group members and thereby respond in a Spirit-led manner to individual needs. Another advantage was that leading together reinforced to the participants the principle of a husband and wife working together as a team.

Unfortunately, the concept of working together isn't very popular in our "Be your own person" culture. Individualism is revered over teamwork. But we're not taking our pattern of marriage from our culture. In biblical marriages, we begin to build dependence on our spouses. God made us to need one another, to trust one another, and to work together for common goals. Often, you'll see a couple that looks extremely successful, but they're really two individuals doing their own thing. They may each be successful, but there is no teamwork. We believe teamwork is at the core of a truly biblical marriage.

Eventually, we were privileged to start over 450 Bible discussion groups on marriage led by laymen. Honestly, it was tough work. God used teamwork between us to accomplish this. Our teamwork wasn't always perfect, especially at first. Because God was changing lives, we were Satan's target.

There was tremendous temptation to criticize one another under pressure. But once we had learned how to honor and encourage one another, our work together was truly effective. You are likely to be surprised how effective you can be when working as a team.

Drew: Part of developing a marriage ministry required meeting pastors and telling them about the Bible discussion groups they could use in their church to strengthen marriages. One godly pastor in a nearby town was polite, but declined. "Our church already has too much going on," he explained. "Please phone us if we can ever serve you," I responded.

Back in our town the groups were multiplying. Many young couples who didn't attend any church participated. The mother of the wife of one of these young couples attended that pastor's church. On a visit to her mother, this young couple met the pastor. They told him all about the Bible discussion groups. The next day I got a call from the pastor. "If you can get couples like that into these groups, I want to be involved!" he stated very emphatically. We mailed the materials to him and coached him on the phone. "These groups work best when led by a husband and wife team," I explained. "Please try to work together." "Okay. I got it," he promised.

A couple of months later I received another call from that pastor. His couples' group had gone well. And he had something additional to report. "My wife always supported my ministry," he explained. "She made food and attended the classes I taught. But when we team-taught this Bible discussion together, it was different. This is the first time we actually ministered together. And I found out that my wife is great [in ministry]!" He went on to describe how much fun it was and how well the couples in the group responded. Clearly, he had discovered a wonderful resource in his own wife. This pastoral couple illustrated Christ and the church to those around them by their teamwork.

Trusting God for a ministry together will take your relationship to a higher level and leave a lasting legacy. Everyone who has led a Bible study knows that the teacher always learns the most. In fact, in our walk with Christ, we've discovered that a person can only mature so far without being obedient to minister to others. And so it is in our relationship as a couple. We can only go so far until we are willing to reach out to others.

Finally, any ministry can lead to doubt and discouragement. The Bible says, "Two are better than one because they have a good return for their labor. For if either of them falls, the one will lift up his companion. But woe to the one who falls when there is not another to lift him up. Furthermore, if two lie down together they keep warm, but how can one be warm alone?" (Ecclesiastes 4:9-11) This verse has been applied to many teamwork situations. But it is particularly relevant to marriage. Look at the last part: "If two lie down together they keep warm." With whom do you want to keep warm?

A Case Study—Speaking Together

Drew: In truth, we were both mediocre speakers as individuals. I frequently got my tongue twisted, lost my place, and talked above the audience's heads. Kit tended to give too many details while the audience fell asleep.

Because leading the small groups together had worked so well, we started speaking as a team. We found a dynamic that appealed and communicated to audiences. I told humorous stories that entertained and engaged the couples. Kit demonstrated a caring attitude and conveyed practical information God could use to change lives. Together we became very effective speakers.

Men still do most of the speaking in churches and at Christian events. In some segments of Christianity, speaking is exclusively reserved for males. More women are exercising their communication gifts in churches and other spiritual venues. However, only very rarely do we see a husband and wife speaking together.

Various justifications are given, possibly that people from some backgrounds would object to a woman speaker. Our purpose speaking together was not to flaunt anybody's interpretation of Scripture. Rather we did so because it was an extraordinarily effective dynamic, especially in marriage ministry. Whenever anyone questioned us about our style, we simply explained that Kit was not preaching or exercising authority. Rather, under the authority of her husband, Kit was sharing principles about marriage that had worked in her own life. With this explanation, every type of group received us and loved what we shared.

Another justification we hear for not speaking together is, "She (or he) doesn't want to speak." This may be true. Public speaking is often reported as the number one fear of many people. However, we've also heard this as an excuse from confident speakers who couldn't share the spotlight with their less well-spoken spouses. Whether or not this is the case, getting a reluctant partner to speak well is usually a matter of encouragement and patience. We have trained couples to speak together all over the world. You would be surprised at who blossoms when given the chance to do so.

In our case, neither one of us *wanted* to speak. We did so because it was the most effective means of expanding a local lay ministry to families. In the beginning, each of us leaned on the other's strengths. Eventually, both of us improved as individuals and yet maintained a dynamic together that was much better than either of us could be as individuals. We've spoken in hundreds of churches and at events all over the US and in 39 other countries. Many listeners, long after forgetting everything specific we said, remember the biblical picture of a husband and wife working together as a team.

HAVING FUN
together

Some people are naturally more fun than others. If not careful, I (Drew) can settle into grim purpose. But I've discovered that being a fun person is a skill that God can develop. Having fun is good for a marriage. Some may say, "Jesus didn't tell His disciples to have fun." Maybe not explicitly, but He apparently did set an example of having fun and was even criticized for it. In Matthew 11:18–19, Jesus contrasts his lifestyle of "eating and drinking" to the more austere life of John the Baptist.

Marriages that are more than ordinary work at having fun together. If you're having fun together, you're serving God because you're investing in your relationship.

Indulging the Other

All people have idiosyncrasies, hobbies, or quirky preferences that bring them joy. Indulging your spouse's special whims can bring fun to your marriage. Ephesians 4:32 says, "Be kind to one another." Indulgence is a form of kindness.

Kit: Drew and I do a lot of fun things together, but one thing he does just for me is based on Deuteronomy 25:4, "You shall not muzzle the ox while he is threshing." While the ox worked, threshing out the grain, it wasn't muzzled so that it could eat some of the grain that fell to the ground. As Drew and I worked hard to build a life together, I wanted to eat some of the "grain" along the way. Only, I prefer my grain to come in the form of surprises. Bringing flowers home to your wife is sure to tell her how important she is to you. Maybe that's because flowers are frivolous. They are alive one day and dead the next. No reason to give them, except, "I love you and appreciate your hard work."

Another thing Drew did, my personal favorite, was to hide money around the house. Now that's fun. There's just something about standing in the grocery line and finding an extra twenty-dollar bill in my purse. Or going to the freezer to decide for the 363rd time what we're going to have for dinner and finding some cool cash. It says, "I'm thinking of you and appreciate your efforts." It breaks the routine. It says to me, "Let's take some time out and have some fun."

Hopefully a married couple knows each other better than anyone else. Each spouse is uniquely qualified to indulge the other.

Drew: Kit and I live on a hobby farm in the country. Although we do maintain large gardens, harvest firewood, and raise fish on our property, our place is more of a tiny wildlife refuge than a farm. We have virtually every form of wildlife. They can be pests. Deer get in the garden and eat the shrubbery. Canadian geese poop on our porch. River otters eat our fish. Beavers cut down favorite trees. Coyotes prowl, looking for our pet cats. Skunks dig up flower beds. Hawks kill our cottontail bunnies. To me the unpredictability of wildlife adds an extra dimension to our lives. Kit indulges me by putting up with the menagerie.

Romance

The top need of most women is to be loved. Romance is one way to express love. There are those three little words that a woman is dying to hear. Those three little words that will set her heart aflutter: "Let's eat out!"

Kit: This may sound silly to some husbands, but women

want a little romance in life. Our lives are filled with a lot of routine activities. We do many of the same things repeatedly! We need a little pizzazz, a little adventure. Most women are starved for it. Why do you think they sell hundreds of millions of romance novels a year? Women want romance!

The written word goes a long way toward romance. Let's say a special occasion is coming up. You can go to the store and spend a lot of money on a card and sign it, and your wife will appreciate that. Or you can take a blank piece of notebook paper and write down how you feel about this special person you married. The notebook paper will win every time. The little things say to your wife, "You're just as precious to me as you were the day I married you."

Passion

Not surprisingly, sex is important to men and women. Sex won't sustain a marriage. Friendship and purpose sustain a marriage. But sex is very important in marriage.

We had a reception for a famous football coach, a godly man who shared a personal story. He and his wife had been intimate and remained lying in bed. She started asking some questions. "Coach," (that's how he shared it) "what would you do if your assistants were letting the backfield players miss their assignments?" He answered, "I guess I'd get them a book on coaching, make them read it, and ask questions to make sure they understood." His wife then replied, "Coach, get yourself a book!"

Christian bookstores have biblical books that encompass the entire sexual relationship and how to maximize God's gift to us as a couple. We shouldn't settle for mediocrity in our sexual relationship.

Drew: Wives do not always need to meet their husband at the door dressed in nothing but cellophane. Husbands don't always have to kidnap their wives away from work to a romantic bed and breakfast. But when we occasionally do special things for each other, that adds a lot of zest to our entire relationship.

When traveling overseas we take a lot of trains. When we can get on a sleeper train, Kit always makes that a special evening. There is just something about that clackety-clack. And now whenever I even see a train, I feel good.

We encourage you not to settle for mediocrity in this vital area of your relationship. Never be ashamed of having fun together. God wants you to.

co-dependency

"Co-dependency?" This word makes couples who rely on each other sound like drug addicts. But the more than ordinary marriage we're talking about might be labeled as co-dependent by today's standards. Independence is revered in our culture. The baby boomer generation was the first to be raised on the idea of individual self-fulfillment. Those attitudes have borne fruit in our society, and that fruit is rotten. The reason is because this kind of lifestyle is completely centered on self. *How will this affect me? What will I get out of it? I have my rights, you know!* We've come to believe we deserve to be happy, and if we're not, then someone is to blame. And in marriage, who is the closest to blame? Most have come to believe that individual happiness is more valuable than the relationship.

But God created us to need each other. In a more than ordinary marriage, two individuals become one person. As already discussed, we each have different God-given strengths. Co-dependency includes relying on your spouse's strengths and developing understanding.

Perhaps you've noticed that couples who live together for a long time seem to look alike. When meeting a long-married couple, you might think, "Did he marry his sister?" Many people judge attractiveness by their own appearance, so for a couple to look somewhat alike isn't uncommon. But many couples who have lived together a long time seem alike because they have evolved in their understanding of each other and have formed a similar approach to life. This can even carry over into their gestures, demeanor, and overall appearance, but it goes deeper than just looks.

A Private Language

Maybe you're familiar with the communication tool called "word pictures." The idea is to help your spouse see how you feel about something by comparing it to something in their sphere of experience.

> Kit: I don't know about you, but I like to shop. And when I've been out for a day of shopping, I want to come home and tell Drew all about it. I want to tell him about my favorite store having a three-day sale that I didn't even know about! I want to tell him about the bargain rack in the back of the store with one

dress in my size. I want to tell him where I went for lunch and I want him to "ooh and aah" over everything I brought home. And I want him to be excited. His usual response is a yawn.

So I found something that makes Drew feel the same way I do about shopping. For Drew, that's fishing. When Drew goes for a day of fishing, he wants to tell me all about it. He wants to tell me about the fishiest place he found on the lake. He wants to show me the fishing lure he's had since high school that caught the big one. He wants to tell me how he out-foxed the fish. And of course, he wants me to be excited about the fish he brings home. Like, "Oh, fish! We won't starve!"

Fishing and shopping create the same feeling. Using word pictures has helped us listen better and share in each other's joy. Now when I bring home a new dress, I just hold it up to myself and say, "Look, Drew, it's a bass!"

A term we call "drawing blood" is also part of our private language. Giving blood is an excruciating process for small-veined Kit. For us, the term "drawing blood" has taken on the meaning of unpleasantness by drawing or taking the fun out of a promise.

Drew: Maybe Kit comes to me with a proposal to go to a movie. I'm busy in the garden and murmur, "Okay." She checks the ads, picks a romantic tear-jerker, and reminds me when we need to leave in order to be on time. Not being finished in the garden, I've changed my mind about going. But I don't want to break my promise. I respond, "Now? I meant when the next Star Wars sequel comes out." Or maybe I've promised to go shopping with her. As the time approaches, I start to hint, "If we weren't going shopping, I could finish that project." Or if I've agreed to attend a ballet, I might say, "If we weren't going to the ballet, we could do anything but go to the ballet." In these examples, I'm not actually breaking my promise. Rather, I'm exacting a little revenge, taking some of the fun away. Now when one of us attempts this, the other says, "You're drawing blood."

We have many other private descriptive terms. They communicate emotions and allow us to quickly understand each other.

Drew: And when it comes to looking like each other, I wish I did look like Kit. Even in her sixties, she is really cute.

46

Enjoying Moments Together

Living in Africa taught us that prosperity isn't necessary to ex- perience joy. Most Africans, for example, can find joy despite poverty in the simple moments of life: sharing a meal, visiting a friend, or singing. People in Jesus' time also had difficult circumstances. To them Jesus said, "For this reason I say to you, do not worry about your life, as to what you will eat; nor for your body, as to what you will put on." (Luke 12:22)

In a wide variety of circumstances, we make a deliberate effort to remind each other, "Enjoy the moment." These moments are something unique to us. Something we share together. They draw us together in a shared memory. Philippians 3:13 is widely misinterpreted. The words "forgetting what lies behind" don't mean Paul abandoned his memories. Rather, Paul is determining to not let his past failures influence his future. In many other places, Paul recites the past for encouragement and instruction.

> What parents don't have photos of their children dis- played in their homes? Pictures remind parents of their victory of love and the joy of those children. When Joshua led Israel across the River Jordan to enter the Promised Land, he issued an unusual instruction. He told each tribe to take a stone for a monument. "These stones are to be a memorial to the people of Isra- el forever." (Joshua 4:7) The memorial reminded the people of the miracles God had done, strengthened their faith, and helped them to conquer the land. In our home, we have enlarged photos and mementos of

significant God-given moments in our lives. Victories of faith and love. These reminders strengthen our faith and assure us of God's purpose in our lives.[1] (Coons, *More Than Ordinary Challenges*)

Couples who are more than ordinary can enjoy moments together and relish those moments through shared memories.

Dealing with Challenges

Life brings trouble. Being married means sharing it. Many couples have experienced troubles from outside of marriage that have made life more difficult—things like sickness, parental responsibilities, or financial pressure. Co-dependent couples help each other in those challenges. In addition to those major sources of trouble, we also face the challenge of everyday trials and tribulations.

> Kit: I've learned a lot of different lessons going through trials and tribulations, but one thing that I've learned comes from a favorite TV character. Andy Griffith's character Matlock always said, "Ain't nothing ever easy." Sounds simple, but it holds a lot of truth. One of our big problems in marriage is that we don't anticipate the certainty of difficulties and problems. We have bought the idea that life is easy, that nothing bad will ever happen to us.

We have faced tragedies and challenges in our married life. *More Than Ordinary Challenges: Dealing with the Unexpected* contains our story about dealing with the heartbreak of infertility. However, the mini-book is about more than infertility. It's about dealing with life when things don't work out as we had hoped due to any challenge.

Many heartwarming stories share about difficult situations that worked out miraculously or through a person's iron-willed determination. The stories are useful in that they inspire hope. But sometimes life just doesn't work out that way. What do we do in a situation that seems unfair?[1] (Coons, *More Than Ordinary Challenges*)

More Than Ordinary Faith: Why Does God Allow Suffering? gives God's biblical purposes to answer the "why" question. The mini-book also explains how we can bring unnecessary suffering on ourselves. More importantly, the text gives biblical responses that can lessen suffering.

Why does God allow suffering? This is a universal question in every culture and in every heart. And the question is reasonable and valid. Lack of a meaningful answer is a barrier to the faith of many. Shallow answers can undermine faith. Fortunately, the Bible gives clear reasons that God allows suffering.[2] (Coons, *More Than Ordinary Faith*)

WILL YOUR MARRIAGE BE
more than ordinary?

A young graduate of an agricultural college went to work for the county agricultural agent. He organized a seminar for the local farmers. "Farm twice as well as you do now," the young agent promised in the invitation. But to his dismay, not one farmer came to the meeting. Later he asked an older farmer, "Why didn't you come? Didn't you want to know how to farm twice as well?" The farmer answered, "Son, I'm not farming half as well as I know how now."

Most of us *know* how to have a better marriage already. The issue is whether we have a commitment to putting what we know into practice. If so, we can work together to develop a common plan. Many sources give a plan that can make a marriage successful. But we think God would have us to move beyond just a successful marriage. In a more than ordinary marriage, each person brings the best out of the other. We've talked about serving sacrificially, giving genuine encouragement, honoring, practicing dynamic teamwork, having fun together, and even embracing co-dependency. As we said in the first paragraph, applying these principles can give us the type of relationship that causes others to ask, "What makes their marriage so special?" Such a relationship truly honors God and can draw others to Him.

Our challenge to you is to take a chance. Trust God for a more than ordinary marriage. And use that relationship to serve our Lord. A more than ordinary marriage doesn't just happen. First a choice is required. The choice is to make the commitment and put in the effort to have that kind of relationship.

> Every moment separates our lives into before and after. Some moments divide our lives into never before and always after. Many of those life-changing moments are based on the choices we make. God allows us to make choices through free will. Most awake moments include minor decisions. Some decisions are more consequential and will affect the remainder of our lives.[3] (Coons, *More Than Ordinary Choices*)

Bibliography

1. Coons, Kit and Drew, *More Than Ordinary Challenges: Dealing with the Unexpected,* 2018

2. Coons, Kit and Drew, *More Than Ordinary Faith: Why Does God Allow Suffering?,* 2018

3. Coons, Kit and Drew, *More Than Ordinary Choices: Making Good Decisions,* 2018

What is a more than ordinary life?

Each person's life is unique and special. In that sense, there is no such thing as an ordinary life. However, many people yearn for lives more special: excitement, adventure, romance, purpose, character. Our site is dedicated to the premise that any life can be more than ordinary.

At **MoreThanOrdinaryLives.com** you will find:

- inspiring stories
- ideas and resources
- entertaining novels
- free downloads

https://morethanordinarylives.com/

Challenge Series

by Kit and Drew Coons

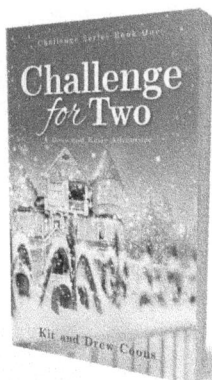

Challenge for Two
Book One

A series of difficult circumstances have forced Dave and Katie Parker into early retirement. Searching for new life and purpose, the Parkers take a wintertime job house sitting an old Victorian mansion. The picturesque river town in southeastern Minnesota is far from the climate and culture of their home near the Alabama Gulf Coast.

But dark secrets sleep in the mansion. A criminal network has ruthlessly intimidated the community since the timber baron era of the 19th century. Residents have been conditioned to look the other way.

The Parkers' questions about local history and clues they discover in the mansion bring an evil past to light and create division in the small community. While some fear the consequences of digging up the truth, others want freedom from crime and justice for victims. Faced with personal threats, the Parkers must decide how to respond for themselves and for the good of the community.

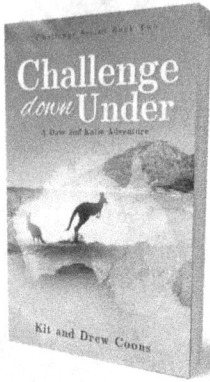

Challenge Down Under
Book Two

Dave and Katie Parker's only son, Jeremy, is getting married in Australia. In spite of initial reservations, the Parkers discover that Denyse is perfect for Jeremy and that she's the daughter they've always wanted. But she brings with her a colorful and largely dysfunctional Aussie family. Again Dave and Katie are fish out of water as they try to relate to a boisterous clan in a culture very different from their home in South Alabama.

After the wedding, Denyse feels heartbroken that her younger brother, Trevor, did not attend. Details emerge that lead Denyse to believe her brother may be in trouble. Impressed by his parents' sleuthing experience in Minnesota, Jeremy volunteers them to locate Trevor. Their search leads them on an adventure through Australia and New Zealand.

Unfortunately, others are also searching for Trevor, with far more sinister intentions. With a talent for irresponsible chicanery inherited from his family, Trevor has left a trail of trouble in his wake and has been forced into servitude. Can Dave and Katie locate him in time?

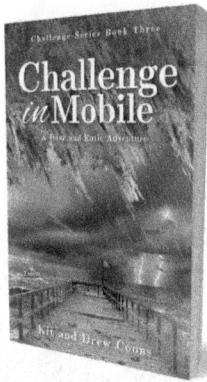

Challenge in Mobile
Book Three

Dave and Katie Parker regret that their only child Jeremy, his wife Denyse, and their infant daughter live on the opposite side of the world. Unexpectedly, Jeremy calls to ask his father's help finding an accounting job in the US. Katie urges Dave to do whatever is necessary to find a job for Jeremy near Mobile. Dave's former accounting firm has floundered since his departure. The Parkers risk their financial security by purchasing full ownership of the struggling firm to make a place for Jeremy.

Denyse finds South Alabama fascinating compared to her native Australia. She quickly resumes her passion for teaching inner-city teenagers. Invited by Katie, other colorful guests arrive from Australia and Minnesota to experience Gulf Coast culture. Aided by their guests, Dave and Katie examine their faith after Katie receives discouraging news from her doctors.

Political, financial, and racial tensions have been building in Mobile. Bewildering financial expenditures of a client create suspicions of criminal activity. Denyse hears disturbing rumors from her students. A hurricane from the Gulf of Mexico exacerbates the community's tensions. Dave and Katie are pulled into a crisis that requires them to rise to a new level of more than ordinary.

More from Kit and Drew Coons

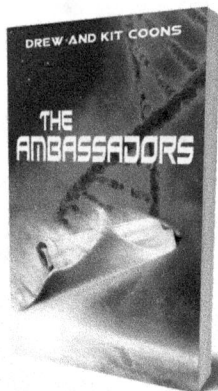

The Ambassadors

Two genetically engineered beings unexpectedly arrive on Earth. Unlike most extraterrestrials depicted in science fiction, the pair is attractive, personable, and telegenic—the perfect talk show guests. They have come to Earth as ambassadors bringing an offer of partnership in a confederation of civilizations. Technological advances are offered as part of the partnership. But humans must learn to cooperate among themselves to join.

Molly, a young reporter, and Paul, a NASA scientist, have each suffered personal tragedy and carry emotional baggage. They are asked to tutor the ambassadors in human ways and to guide them on a worldwide goodwill tour. Molly and Paul observe as the extraterrestrials commit faux pas while experiencing human culture. They struggle trying to define a romance and partnership while dealing with burdens of the past.

However, mankind finds implementing actual change difficult. Clashing value systems and conflicts among subgroups of humanity erupt. Inevitably, rather than face difficult choices, fearmongers in the media start to blame the messengers. Then an uncontrolled biological weapon previously created by a rogue country tips the world into chaos. Molly, Paul, and the others must face complex moral decisions about what being human means and the future of mankind.

more than
ORDINARY
lives
MINI SERIES

More Than Ordinary Challenges—
Dealing with the Unexpected

More Than Ordinary Marriage—
A Higher Level

More Than Ordinary Faith—
Why Does God Allow Suffering?

More Than Ordinary Wisdom—
Stories of Faith and Folly

More Than Ordinary Abundance—
From Kit's Heart

More Than Ordinary Choices—
Making Good Decisions

more than
ORDINARY
lives

Visit **https://morethanordinarylives.com/**
for more information.

About the Authors

Kit and Drew Coons met while Christian missionaries in Africa in 1980. As humorous speakers specializing in strengthening relationships, they have taught in every part of the US and in thirty-nine other countries. For two years, the Coonses lived and served in New Zealand and Australia. They are keen cultural observers and incorporate their many adventures into their writing. Kit and Drew are unique in that they speak and write as a team.

www.ingramcontent.com/pod-product-compliance
Lightning Source LLC
Chambersburg PA
CBHW060537030426
42337CB00021B/4304